Hidden Treasure

Hidden Treasure

Unlocking God's Word

A series of short expositions and applications

Volume 1

Robert Iannuccilli

OnScribe Media

Hidden Treasure
Unlocking God's Word
A series of short expositions and applications: Volume 1
Robert Iannuccilli
Copyright © 2012

Published by OnScribe Media
www.onscribemedia.com

All Scripture quotations unless otherwise indicated, are taken from the King James Version of the Bible (KJV).

Publisher's Cataloging-in-Publication Data

Iannuccilli, Robert, 1957-
    Hidden treasure: unlocking god's word: a series of short expositions and applications: volume 1/ written by Robert Iannuccilli - 1st ed.

    p. cm.
    includes index.

ISBN 978-0-9852570-0-2

    1. Bible.   2. Devotional literature
I. Bible. II. Title. III. Series.

Library of Congress Control Number (LCCN): 2012904803

Cover Design: Ignite

Printed in the United States of America
First Edition 2012

This book is dedicated to the loving memory of my dad, Joseph, who, just before his passing, while I was yet in a difficult phase of my life, held out high hopes that I would again make him proud, and to my beloved brother Steve, who, before his untimely death, was instrumental in rescuing me from a horrible place.

I love and at times miss you both terribly.

Contents

Contents (continued)

Acknowledgements

First, I recognize that without certain, precious people, (too numerous and personal to mention here) this book would not be. These are those who stood by me and believed in me in the not too distant past, through the darkest period of my life; a time in which I was not my true self and had lost my way. You may be unaware, but your love, loyalty, dedication, faith, prayers and abiding confidence have deeply impacted my destiny.

Further, I am deeply appreciative of the body of believers at Faith On Fire, the group I now pastor, for their love, loyalty, and dedication. These truths were first given you in my often long-winded messages. Your encouragement and reception of my ministry have been a source of motivation in my writing. Without you, none of this could have transpired. I consider it an honor and privilege to be called "pastor" by many of you.

Particularly, I thank Tom Mortimer of Praise Tabernacle for his time, talent, endless words of encouragement and labor of love in editing the entire manuscript. Also, thanks to Jared Iannuccilli, (my son) and his company, Ignite, for their overall assistance in implementing this undertaking; from cover design, layout and every particular.

Additionally, with a warmed heart, I lovingly acknowledge my three children, Jared, Meredith and Joy for never giving up on me and always believing that I would stand tall again; as well as my dear "bride," Barbara, for remaining by my side and filling my days with smiles and joy.

Finally and mostly I give my highest praises to the one who saved me and never has let go of me. My life is so much more a testament to His love, forbearance and faithfulness than any qualities inherent in me. I stand amazed at Him with whom I have to do and I thank Him for allowing me the privilege of representing Him in any fashion whatsoever.

Hidden Treasure:
A Wealth of Scriptural Insights

Preface

The pages that follow are born out of an intense love for the Word of God and a belief that, through His written word, God's voice can be heard. God speaks for Himself through the book He has given us. Our minds are renewed and union with Christ is established through biblical understanding, insight and application. In my 35 years of biblical study and ministry, with a passion to know God, I have developed a great love for good Christian books. My personal Biblical library presently consists of thousands of volumes.

I have often thought of putting my own pen to the page, but being the perfectionist that I am, have repeatedly put off any efforts until now. Part of the reason for this delay seems to have been my inability to decide upon a subject or a type of book to write. I have come to the conclusion that writing a devotional work would give occasion to touch on a great variety of topics and to comment on a host of scripture. Besides, devotional works have always been a personal favorite of mine and have given me the seeds to many of my messages.

My hope here is not to merely throw another devotional book into the mix, but to fill a void I have found in most Christian literature. My experience in reading published Christian works is that much of them are so scholarly as to be unintelligible and impractical to the average Christian. At other times, the books are so general, shallow and self-serving that they lose touch with the biblical text.

My goal is to express the essence of the scriptures that I have chosen in a way that will give clarity to the biblical text, while touching and enhancing the spiritual lives of its readers. I have ever been an advocate of endeavoring to keep the relation of the Spirit and the Word intact. The two are inextricably bound together and must never be separated. The Spirit speaks and ministers out of the Word and the Spirit ever confirms and brings focus back to the Word. Another way of saying it would be that the Word brings us the Spirit and the Spirit brings us back to the Word as confirmation. He, being the third person of the Trinity, will never speak of (or draw attention to) Himself, but will always, in unison and in harmony with the Godhead, draw the believer to Jesus, as well as glorify Him.

Finally, I trust these pages, while not meaning to be a substitute for the reading of God's Word, will in fact, inspire its readers to cultivate a greater interest in the revelation God has given us and a greater appreciation of His unspeakable gift: Jesus Christ.

I also want to give a special thanks to all who have valued my insight and passion. Many have continually urged me to do what I have been reluctant to do: commit some of my thoughts to writing. May you, the reader of these pages, be blessed and encouraged by the Spirit and the Word as you read the scriptures and the comments that I share herein.

Respectfully Yours and Entirely His,
Pastor Robert Iannuccilli
Faith On Fire Ministries
www.faithonfire.us

This Is The Day

"The stone which the builders refused is become the head stone of the corner. This is the lord's doing; it is marvelous in our eyes. This is the day which the Lord hath made; we will rejoice and be glad in it. Save now, I beseech thee, O Lord: O Lord, I beseech thee, send now prosperity."

(Psalm 118:22-25)

The rejoicing spoken of here is not merely an unwarranted developing of a positive mental attitude; an unfounded call to an optimistic outlook on life. It is not something we are summoned to initiate. Rather, the rejoicing and gladness here signified is in response to an understanding and reception of something that the Lord has done.

The "day the Lord hath made" is not a general reference to just any day, but to a specific "day." It specifically refers to what the bible calls "the day of the Lord;" the day God comes to save His own. It is a reference to God's gracious and wonderful activity in bringing us salvation.

This passage is a clear reference to the ministry of Christ from His incarnation to His glorification and intercession. More precisely and specifically, "this day" makes reference to the moment Jesus cried, "It is finished" (John 19:30), signifying the accomplishment of our salvation and the securing of our blessing.

It is not at first an allusion to some present day, but a look to a specific day in the past. It speaks not of this day that the Lord is giving in the present, but of a day in the past when the Lord has acted on behalf of His own. Yet, for all this, note that it is not called "that day" as to speak of some remote time when God one time acted, but carries present meaning and impact so as to effect our present day and lives.

The "day" then comes to signify the entire era, from the time of that achievement to the time of His second coming. It is not merely a reference to a single day. Though it all began on a single day, it has continuing consequences and wondrous benefits. It is, in fact, an era or an age; a lasting and sustained period of divine grace and favor; a prolonged season when God's people can count fully on the Lord's constant and continued willingness to save, deliver and bless.

> Adam gave us a day of sadness, but Christ has given us, instead, a day of gladness

This is called "the Lord's doing" and is said to be "marvelous." It is the Lord's doing as opposed to anything we could have done. This is the reason for the exultation, "We will rejoice and be glad in it." Indeed, Adam gave us a day of sadness, but Christ has given us, instead, a day of gladness! The Lord Himself said, "Your father Abraham rejoiced to see my day; and he saw it, and was glad." (John 8:56)

What else should we do? Having obtained so great a deliverance through our Savior and having seen the eternal mercy of God so brilliantly displayed, should we then murmur and doubt? Should despair and a sense of defeat fill our hearts when God has gone to such an extent to make His life and gifts to be ours? Should we question the One who has set in motion every blessing on our behalf and demonstrated His willingness to assist and favor us today? No, let confidence and joy characterize your demeanor as you rejoice all the daylong on the grounds of what He has done. With the psalmist, let us boldly call upon Him, saying, "Save now" and "Send now prosperity."

May this wondrous scripture set the tone for each day of the year. No matter how this day may appear or what it is that you feel and face, be reminded of what He has ordered for you so that you might declare, "This is the day that the Lord hath made; we will rejoice and be glad in it!"

———•+•———

Speaking To Yourself

"For she said within herself, 'If I may but touch His garment, I shall be made whole'... thy faith hath made thee whole."

(Matthew 9:21-22)

*A*ll three of the synoptic gospels (Matthew, Mark and Luke) record this miracle of the woman whose long-standing infirmity of twelve years was cleared up instantaneously. In each of these accounts, Jesus attributes the victory to her faith. This is not to say that faith was the grounds for her miracle, but rather the means to her blessing. Indeed, the grounds for all God's blessings are His goodness, willingness, grace and power. Apart from these, no confidence or optimism on the part of any could procure a change.

So then, the basis of all our hope is the love and goodness of God who has promised and instituted so great a salvation on our behalf. Need we be reminded that no goodness within us has initiated the work of God in our lives? We mustn't look to ourselves as being the grounds for blessing, but to His inherent and absolute graciousness.

Yet, while we insist upon God's willingness and power as the root of all bounty, we must not expect these, in and of themselves, to produce the much-desired fruit of His manifest goodness. Our faith is to be the hand by which we lay hold and avail ourselves of the desired blessing.

Here, the Lord counts the faith of the woman as the key to the manifestation of God's power. In saying "thy faith has made thee whole," our Lord takes the crown from His own head and places it upon hers.

Today's text tells us what it was that transpired within this woman that brought about the reversal of her misfortune. The key is what "she said within herself." By continually saying to herself, "If I may but touch the hem of his garment, I shall be made whole," she exalted Jesus' might, goodness and love over every barrier to blessing in her life.

> Faith moves God and God moves in response to faith.

She overcomes every thought of condemnation and reluctance on the part of God and she stirs herself to trust Him. She persists in believing and mounts up upon the wings of faith. As moments pass, she surmounts every notion of disappointment and rises to complete and assured confidence. In the original, the text literally reads, "she kept on saying within herself." She rehearsed and rested upon God's willingness and ability. She soon goes from saying to knowing. She stands in a steadfast foreknowledge of assured blessing. She knows that the miracle is to be hers.

Her confidence was complete and pleasing to Christ. Her touching Him resulted in His touching her. The miraculous had been granted. The blessing was so vast that she may have thought of herself the same as those who dream, but this was no dream. The impossible had become reality.

Faith moves God and God moves in response to faith. Without faith it is impossible to please Him, but by faith we may be assured of His manifest blessing. In the end, it is not only what He says that determines the victory, it is also what we say in response to Him that actually secures the promise. What, right now, are you saying within yourself? This is no time to doubt. It is your hour to believe. God has spoken. May you believe Him now!

———•◆•———

Come

"Come unto me... and I will give you..."
(Matthew 11:28)

What words of comfort and promise this verse contains. Here many have found the provision of the very peace and rest they pursued.

So rich is our text that it will suffice us today to concentrate on that single word, "Come." The Gospel brings to us a word of invitation, not rejection. "Come unto me," Jesus says; He does not say depart from me. "I will give you" is His promise; He does not say I will take from you or withhold from you or even demand of you. Come just as you are, bringing nothing but your tiredness, your heaviness, your emptiness and your hopelessness is His plea. That we come, not improve, is His first concern. If you cannot come with faith, then come for faith. If you cannot come with repentance, then come for repentance. If you cannot come with a warm heart, then come that your heart might be warmed. Come empty-handed, discouraged, defeated or broken, but come! Come condemned or ruined and He will receive you.

The victory lies in understanding to whom it is that we are invited to come. In coming to Christ, we are not coming to one who is undecided about us. It is He that has come to us, before we ever gave thought of coming to Him. We are His commission and assignment. His willingness is not in question. He is not just sympathetic toward our concern; He is powerful on our behalf. He does not merely say, "Come and I will understand or sympathize," but He says, "Come and I will give." He receives all comers, so that He might bless all that come, regardless of their need or condition.

What would we think of a doctor who has a reputation of leaving all of his patients in the finest condition after he treats them, only to find out that he will only treat those who are faring well before they are permitted to see him? Would not such a practitioner's ability be brought into question? Would not such a physician's compassion and capability be considered spurious? We do not have a physician who is called "great" by His handling of those that are whole. No, He seeks-out and welcomes the most dismal of cases and the most hopeless of causes to demonstrate His gracious abilities.

> If you cannot come with faith, then come for faith

I see in this word "come," a challenge to put Him to the test. He never fails. When nothing else can help, the Lord will improve your condition. May you "come," both now and boldly, to the Great Restorer of your soul, to find mercy full and strength outpoured. For they that come to Him, He will in no way dismiss or fail. His purpose for you coming to Him is so that you might come and never leave, but be fully and completely satisfied and blessed.

The Rest Is Up To Him

"Come unto me, all ye that labour and are heavy laden, and I will give you rest. Take my yoke upon you, and learn of me; for I am meek and lowly in heart: and ye shall find rest unto your souls."
(*Matthew 11:28*)

I heard a story of a minister who came to the home of a very poor woman with the intention of giving her help. Arriving with money in hand, he came to the door and knocked, but received no answer. Some time later, he ran into the woman in the marketplace and explained to her how he had come to her home with the good intention of offering her assistance. With that, the woman told the good minister that she had heard him and was quite sorry she did not answer. She assumed it was the landlord again, coming for the rent.

The Gospel ("Good News") does not concern itself with what we have to give to God, but with what He has to bring to us. Jesus, here, does not come demanding that which is due Him, but offering relief to an overly taxed people. His compassionate eye is directed toward those who, through hardship, are toiling to advance themselves and improve their own condition. He sees them in their struggle and understands the crushing weight under which they labor. He perceives the weariness brought upon them by the cares they carry. To those who sense themselves in this condition, He offers relief. He brings to bear upon the storm-tossed, heavily burdened, and strained life, His rest. Here is a peaceful haven to which we may come and a tranquility that we may possess. Here is a divine strengthening of the soul. Jesus comes to us with much more than a sympathetic concern for our weariness; He comes with a remedy for our infirmity.

Indeed, it is here that most miss it. We are quite confused about God. Many imagine that God is the cause of their misfortune and struggles. Here, Jesus summons us to learn otherwise. This knowledge is not attained through mental achievement, but by association and fellowship with Him. Come, He says, and I will give you rest! Take, He says, and in taking you shall learn (i.e. experience and prove for yourselves) of God's goodness and favor.

> The Gospel does not concern itself with what we give to God

Religion has always been obsessed with adding weights and conditions to an already burdened people. Jesus comes instead to relieve our load.

Heavens assistance is yours today in Jesus Christ. There is no reason to go alone. Come to Him so that He might come to you. Learn from Him so that His rest might be your possession. Drink of His mercy and take of His strength. Feed upon His favor. Walk in victory.

HIDDEN TREASURE

His Yoke: No Joke

"Come unto me, all ye that labour and are heavy laden, and I will give you rest. Take my yoke upon you, and learn of me; for I am meek and lowly in heart: and ye shall find rest unto your souls."
(Matthew 11:28)

In Jesus day, religionists often spoke of taking on the yoke of the law. Essentially, this was a call to an attachment to God's commands. Jesus, here, takes the figure of the "yoke" and speaks of it in an altogether different respect. His yoke is set over against their yoke. While theirs is cumbersome, awkward, heavy and difficult, His is fine fitting, strengthening, relieving and easy.

When people enter business partnerships a yoke is formed. The same is true in marriage. This brings to light the warnings and dangers associated with being "unequally yoked" together. Each party brings something to the relationship with the intention of pooling resources and increasing potential. Ideally, such relationships should be equitable and advantageous, but are often unfavorable when one party brings more to the table than the other.

The yoke is a device used to link animals together so as to create a union between them. The underlying purpose behind the use of the yoke is to pool and share resources. The law of multiplication and impartation then comes into play. The strength of one beast of burden is multiplied by the strength of another; by the adding of resources, the impartation of a new element is achieved.

The religious leaders in Jesus' day, as in our own, were guilty of adding additional pressures and increasing the guilt of an already overtaxed people. The yoke that they put on people's lives was destructive. For this reason, many denounce religion and go without God in their lives. They are handling life's burdens by themselves, often yoking themselves to futile helpers. This leads to a sad, tiresome, poor and lonely existence.

Religion is like tying a dead animal to a living organism

In many ways, religion is like tying a dead animal to a living organism. Imagine an ox not only struggling to pull a large carriage behind it, but also dragging the carcass of another great beast beside it. Often, religion is this great beast! People have enough cares, weights and things to manage and deal with in their lives without adding any additional weight.

Recognizing both our need and condition, Jesus invites us to an attachment to Himself. In so doing, we are granted access to the Supernatural. We are linked to divine supply and assistance. He eases and lightens our load. Here, we find a delightful distribution of the load. He bears most of the weight.

If we would admit it, are we not often a burden to ourselves? This need not dishearten us. He is pleased to carry our burden. He will bear you up. All you need to do is come so that His relief may be yours. Entrust him today with the very care of your soul and the concerns of your life.

———•◦•———

Our Wills And His

"Father, if thou be willing, let this cup pass from me: nevertheless not my will, but thine, be done."
(Luke 22:42)

Traditionally, it has been common to treat the prayer of Jesus in Gethsemane so as to demonstrate His reluctance to face death by way of the cross. However, a careful study of key New Testament passages and concepts supports an alternative understanding. It is evident in many places that Jesus both accepted and embraced the cross as the Father's will and His own mission. In Gethsemane, Jesus was said to be under such a yoke and in such agony that His very sweat was mingled with His own blood. Here, death was threatening Him and appeared imminent. It is in this context, and under these conditions, facing a premature death that He is said to have prayed for the removal of "this cup." Hebrews 5:7 in the NIV reads, "During the days of Jesus' life on earth, He offered up prayers and petitions with loud cries and tears to the one who could save Him from death, and He was heard because of His reverent submission." The cup, and the death Jesus asked to be and was delivered from, was not the cup of sufferings of the cross, but the present "cup" He was experiencing in Gethsemane! Luke, in fact, tells us that angels came in answer to His prayer, strengthening Him.

The point here is that although Jesus believed that His will (to live through Gethsemane) was one with the Father's, He prayed, submitting any purposes of His own to the will of God. Here we learn not merely to submit ourselves to God when our wills are at odds with His, but even when we are certain to be praying and pressing in for the very things God has for us, to ever pray with a spirit of humility, submission and surrender.

The purpose of prayer (and the key to answered prayer) is to pursue and request those things that are in harmony with God's will and purposes for our lives and His kingdom. True prayer, and the confidence that attends it, is not gained when we act so as to attempt to wrestle with God in order to have Him grant our wishes and demands. So long as prayer is the felt expression of our wills it will be weak and uncertain. But when our wills are submitted so as to be in harmony with His, we can plead with an assurance that what we are asking is but that which He wills to give. Here is the ground of boldness with God. Here we can plead and even demand, "Thy kingdom come, Thy will be done."

> The purpose of prayer is to request things in harmony with God's will

The servant is not above his master. If Jesus is willing to relinquish His will and way, should we not be prepared to do the same? Augustine prayed, saying, "Our wills are ours to make them Thine." It was when Abraham fully surrendered his son Isaac that he discovered God was more interested in full ownership of himself than in taking his son from him.

Faith operates best when it is fully founded upon trust; trust that the Lord indeed is good in the greatest sense and that His desire is that we might receive His finest in our lives.

The key here is that our wills and desires must be continually surrendered to Him; otherwise they turn into the ambition and independence which separate us from the very happiness we seek. Today, may you enjoy the peace and power that come only as you surrender your desires to Him, having them refined and returned to you so that you might walk in complete harmony and unity with His will and purpose.

———•◦•———

If You Can't, He Can!

"And ofttimes it hath cast him into the fire, and into the waters, to destroy him: but if thou canst do anything, have compassion on us, and help us. Jesus said unto him, If thou canst believe, all things are possible to him that believeth. And straightway the father of the child cried out, and said with tears, Lord, I believe; help thou mine unbelief."

(Mark 9:22-24)

*W*earied by a demon who persistently and presently seeks to destroy his son, and having already unsuccessfully brought the boy to the disciples of Jesus, this father pleads for assistance from the Lord saying, "If you can do anything... help us." Though the disciples could do nothing at all, the father now queries Christ as to whether He can do anything to relieve the condition. To this inquiry the Lord speedily and abruptly responds, "If you can believe, all things are possible..."

No sooner does the man say, "If you can," that Jesus responds as if to say, "It's not if I can," but "if *you* can." It's not, "Can God?" Of course God can! The question instead is, "Can you?" Can you trust completely that God can? An equally acceptable, alternate rendering of the text further brings this out: Jesus was, quite possibly, sarcastically repeating the man's words back to him to show the absurdity and ridiculous nature of his query. "If you can?" implies that the very idea was preposterous, to which Jesus responds, "BELIEVE; All things are possible to him that believes."

Either way, one thing is for certain: Jesus makes faith the supreme requirement for the miraculous. God moves when He is moved by faith. Without faith it is impossible to please Him. Unbelief is our greatest hindrance to victory.

It appears the man now faces a dual dilemma. On one hand he has a harassed son who can be helped by nothing but faith. On the other hand, he has an unbelieving heart that he cannot mend. No more than he can deliver his son from the demons that surround him, can he free his own heart from the unbelief that fills it.

Faith is the supreme requirement for the miraculous

He is certainly down, but he is not out. Ultimately, he will not leave defeated. He came for mercy and mercy he shall have! He refuses to believe that the answer must ultimately depend on anything about him or within him. He turns it all back on Christ when he says, "Lord, I believe; help my unbelief." We grossly misunderstand these words and his plea if we take them to mean, "Help me to believe so that by my improving I may somehow prevail." No, we get the essence of his meaning only when we realize this man was trusting Christ regardless of anything that could or could not be found within himself. If we imagine he is here praying for his improvement, we then miss the intent and heart of his plea. He is not praying for a change in his unbelieving condition. Instead, he is praying, with confidence so that no unbelieving condition of his own could hinder Christ's gracious ability! He is overcoming his unbelief by ignoring it and focusing on Christ. Here he does not pray about his unbelief. He does not ask for help with his unbelief, but for help in spite of his unbelief. It is as though he says, "Do not require of me what I do not possess. Act, as You are able to act."

Is not this faith in action? May we take our deepest needs to Christ today, not looking for something worthy or deserving in ourselves, but looking only unto His mercy and ability.

———•◦•———

Unbelief: No Hindrance To Faith!

"And straightway the father of the child cried out, and said with tears, Lord, I believe; help thou mine unbelief."

(Mark 9:24)

So important is a proper sense of these words that, at the risk of being redundant, I thought it would be important to comment upon them again.

The increase and victory of faith does not come by our struggle, determination or attempt at improvement. Faith is increased and triumphant by its exercise.

When the disciples asked the Lord to increase their faith, He never did give them lessons on how they should go about improving their ability to believe. In fact, He wouldn't even lend credibility to the notion that it was more faith that they needed. Instead, He drew attention to the fact that small faith could yield great results. He said that if one had faith no larger than a mustard seed (the smallest known seed) and put it to use, it would effectively displace the mountains and uproot the trees. The emphasis here is not upon the need to increase faith, but upon the need to utilize it.

In Mark chapter 9, when this father comes to Jesus desperate over his son's demonized condition, wishing for a miracle, he is brought face to face with the inadequacy of his own spiritual resources. He is now left with but two alternatives: He could go away in despair till the day that he improves his spiritual condition to some qualifying status of believing, or he could take the dual difficulty (that of his boy and that of his unbelief) and cast them both entirely upon Christ, trusting wholly in His mercy and omnipotence. When confronted with his own deficiency, this father was not dissuaded from his conviction that Christ could move on his behalf. Believing Christ was bigger than both his burdens; he exercised his faith and witnessed the miraculous.

> Faith is at its finest when it looks completely away from itself and magnifies and exalts the Lord

Faith is at its finest when it looks completely away from itself and magnifies and exalts the Lord. What this man recognized (and what you and I need to remember) is that faith is about confidence in Christ ONLY and not about any confidence we have in our confidence toward Christ. Faith in ones faith is self-reliance and promises nothing more than discouragement and defeat. We never trust the Savior so little as when we fall back on our own righteousness and efforts.

John Wesley, paraphrasing the text, gives us the best sense of these words. "Though my faith be so small that it is better labeled unbelief, yet help me!" This man was not asking for help with his faith. He was asking for help with his son, despite his struggle with faith! To take it further, I would say, "Such is your ability and willingness that my insufficiency cannot close the door of grace in my life."

May we, with all our inability, deficiency and faithlessness, cast ourselves upon Him who cares for us and trust Him now!

———•◆•———

Ready Or Not?

"Then said He unto him, A certain man made a great supper, and bade many: And sent his servant at supper time to say to them that were bidden, Come; for all things are now ready. And they all with one consent began to make excuse..."

(Luke 14:16-18)

*A*sk nearly any Christian if they would like to enjoy more of God in their lives and they invariably will respond, "Yes, of course!" In theory this may be true, but here Jesus shares an important parable to show how readily people put God off and ignore the things of the Kingdom through a lack of spiritual appetite.

This text is in response to one man's truism, "Blessed is he that shall eat bread in the kingdom of God." The first thing Jesus emphasizes is that the kingdom is not something that will come someday in the distant future, but is, in fact, an already real and present happening. He likens the joys, celebration and benefits of the kingdom to a feast that has been well planned, prepared and paid for. In biblical days, like ours, invitations for special events were published beforehand. Additionally, when the precise time to gather would come, a proclamation would go forth, summoning the guests to draw together and participate in the festivities. Here, Jesus employs this custom to illustrate a certain historical, spiritual and universal truth in relation to the call to kingdom enjoyment. In effect, He says, "Many show a great interest in the things of Heaven so long as there is no pressing, present demand placed upon them, but when the kingdom invitation comes requiring immediate, present and decisive action and response, most people are unwilling to detach themselves from their preoccupations and engage themselves in the things of God."

The truth is that most people are self-satisfied and complacent, feeding on substitutes, having no real room or appetite for spiritual things. In this parable, Jesus gives three examples of typical excuses which exemplify this singular reason for kingdom neglect. The first has to do with earthly fulfillments. Here is a man who is willing to substitute dirt for the spiritual enjoyment of the kingdom! The land he now owns is of greater importance and value to him than the salvation God offers and Christ purchased. This applies to any thing in one's life that distracts from the only thing of supreme importance. It depicts those that seek life and pleasure in all the wrong places. The second relates to business. How many are so preoccupied with making a living that they fail to make a life and ignore the true riches of God's presence and kingdom? The third has to do with social relations. Here is a man giving to his wife what is due to his God! It is interesting here, that while the others ask and pray to be excused,

> Revival is not so much a question of God's willingness as it is of our readiness

this man simply and boldly declares, "I cannot come." How many have sought or prayed for a mate or life partner only to allow their companions to draw them away from God?

We deceive ourselves into imagining that we really do want more of God than we presently possess. The reality is that we have all of God that we currently desire! The kingdom and revival are not so much a question of God's willingness as it is of our readiness. May we today lay aside other things and pursuits to begin a new quest after the things of God.

Got Hunger?

"...Then the master of the house being angry said
to his servant, Go out quickly into the streets and
lanes of the city, and bring in hither the poor, and
the maimed, and the halt, and the blind. And the
servant said, Lord, it is done as thou hast command-
ed, and yet there is room. And the lord said unto
the servant, Go out into the highways and hedges,
and compel them to come in, that my house may be
filled."

(Luke 14:21-23)

These verses serve as a sort of sequel to the parable of
the Great Supper. After the invitation is neglected or
rejected by others, an alternate group is sought out as desir-
able candidates for the kingdom feast. If the first group of in-
vitees will not appreciate and value the prepared feast, then
another sort who will cherish the opportunity to participate
will be given the offer. There are many who will never take
a real and saving interest in the Higher Life. These are the
self-satisfied; those who are feeding and feasting upon earthly pleasures and possessions. These are those who view the
gospel call as an inconvenience, interference or an outright
nuisance. They do not want their lives interrupted by God.
They are quite pleased to continue without Him.

It is often asked, with objection, whether a loving God would send anyone to Hell. The proper answer is that a loving God has provided a way that none should ever go without Him or any of His Joys. This being said, it must also be understood that though God has gone to such lengths to prepare, pay for, and plead for humanity's comfort; if men refuse such privileges, then it must not be God who is to blame that they go without Him. No, God does not send anyone to Hell; men, themselves, choose a life without Him. What makes us think that one who will not enjoy a life on earth with God, would somehow be comfortable in Heaven where He is completely served, honored, and central to all life?

> The Gospel is offered to all, but effectual only for some

In any event, the Gospel is offered to all, but effectual only for some, hence the often misunderstood saying, "many are called but few are chosen." The kind that embrace the gospel most readily are the poor, the downcast, the frowned upon, the lonely, the hurting, the cheated, the broken, i.e. the "needy." Here, Jesus adjures us to go after the "hungry" and the "needy" and compel them to come, enter, and enjoy the exclusive kingdom joys and privileges prepared for His children, but rejected by others.

The emphasis here is on the word "compel." They are to be compelled, persuaded, or convinced by strong argument and pleading, because they will imagine the offer is too good to be true. If the difficulty with the first group is that they *would not* come, then the difficulty with the second group is that they imagine they *could not* come. They deem themselves unworthy and poor candidates for such favor. Jesus said, "Tell them convincingly that I want them, that I'll receive them, and that I'll bless them."

It is encouraging to know that God will receive all that come to Him. He embraces all that desire Him. There are none that He turns away. He rejects only those who reject Him. If you are hungry for God today, then you are well on your way to the feast. All things have been made ready. The gift is free and paid for. May you partake and enjoy it now!

———•+•———

On Second Thought

"But when he saw the wind boisterous, he was afraid;
and beginning to sink, he cried, saying, Lord, save
me. And immediately Jesus stretched forth his hand,
and caught him, and said unto him, O thou of little
faith, wherefore didst thou doubt?"
(Matthew 14:30-31)

Some have criticized Peter for stepping out of the boat to go to Jesus, ascribing this venture to his rash and impetuous nature. Indeed, there was no stampede on the part of the other disciples to get to Christ that day. Agreeably, Peter's desire and decision was highly attributable to his bold and adventurous nature.

It should be remembered however, that Jesus never did say to Peter, "Why did you come?" He only said, "Why did you doubt?" In fact, the Lord Himself said, "Come." The notion that Peter should never have taken this step has "little" foundation in the Word of God. I say little because there is something worth considering here: It is important to think things through before making decisions. We must count the cost before venturing forth and consider the worthiness of our objectives before delving into the deep. The corresponding demand and commitment to faith that is required to pursue a goal should be contemplated before leaping into the dark. This is all a part of the wise decision-making process that is accomplished by thinking things through. Far too many people imagine that faith means a complete disengaging of the mind in all respects!

Here, Jesus attributes the sinking of Peter, not so much to faulty first thoughts, but to costly second thoughts. The word that our Lord uses here for "doubt" is interesting, significant and deserves careful consideration. It literally means, "to think twice". In questioning Peter why it is that he doubted, He is actually asking him why he "thought twice."

Somewhere between getting out of the boat and getting to where Jesus was, Peter allowed "second thoughts" to master him. Having once considered what he was in for, that is, the size of the waves and the measure of the storm, Peter had no more business with the wind, waves or weather at all! Having thought it through, he should have been through with thinking and never again looked to anything but Jesus.

Think it through and be through with thinking

Surely, second thoughts will present themselves, especially if we have given little thought at first to any decision that demands our confidence. The greater the decision, the more likely "second thoughts" will arise, but if we are to walk in faith and win the victory, we must learn to refuse them. Think it through and be through with thinking is sound advice here.

Are you faltering between faith and doubt? Are you consumed with "second thoughts?" Perhaps, if opportunity still exists, you may still return to "safety," or perhaps, that is no longer an option. Oftentimes it is not that a poor decision was made, but that a lack of confidence has prevailed. Fix your eyes upon Jesus today; He is greater than the wind and waves. Christ will show Himself mighty to those who look steadfastly upon Him. Today, may we refuse every competing concern that threatens complete confidence in Him!

———•—•———

Short-Lived Faith

"But when he saw the wind boisterous, he was afraid; and beginning to sink, he cried, saying, Lord, save me. And immediately Jesus stretched forth his hand, and caught him, and said unto him, O thou of little faith, wherefore didst thou doubt?"

(Matthew 14:30-31)

Naturally speaking, no two objects can occupy the same space at the same time. So spiritually, faith and doubt cannot co-exist. Confidence in Christ and second thoughts are mutually exclusive. This is borne out by an understanding of this passage.

By referring to Peter as "Little-Faith" (for in the original Greek, Jesus is assigning a nick-name to Peter) He is not referring to a faith that is mingled with doubt. This is not a reference to the quantity of Peter's faith. He is not referring to Peter's faith as small in size. In fact, Peter's faith in stepping out of the boat and walking on the water was huge, incredible faith (I don't see any of the other disciples making any moves here)! No, Jesus is not calling Peter's faith small. Instead, He is drawing attention to the short-lived nature of Peter's faith. It was small in its duration; the length of time it lasted.

The problem arises when Peter starts looking at the insurmountable odds and difficulties. This is when fear displaces faith in Peter's heart. He goes, in an instant, from the heights of faith to the depths of doubt. He plummets from the pinnacle of full-faith, or all-faith, to the abyss of no-faith in a rapid fashion. Here, "Little-Faith" refers to a faith that begins so well only to fail so miserably. It is a faith that trusts Christ fully, only to be soon overcome and displaced by fear and doubt. The trouble with Peter is not that he hasn't enough faith. His faith is marvelous, as far as it goes. It just doesn't go far enough. His faith is not sustained. It doesn't last. It gives way. Peter does not persevere in faith. He does not stay in faith.

When you study the story, it becomes apparent that the wind and waves did not arise or swell so as to cause Peter to fear. No, the wind and waves were constant long before Peter ever thought of stepping out of the boat. There is no change of circumstance, no new factor, which causes Peter to waver. There is but a change in focus. Beginning with complete concentration and confidence toward Christ, at some point, Peter's attention shifts to the difficulty and dilemma in which he finds himself. Here, faith vacates his heart and fear floods his soul. Here, second thoughts arise. Whereas, at first, Peter is taken up with Christ, at last, he is taken up with the crisis.

Confidence in Christ and second thoughts are mutually exclusive

The precise point of this shift is introduced by the little word "but." "But he saw the wind…!" Here, thoughts begin to arise, thoughts of his own foolishness perhaps; suggestions of devastation flood his soul. Christ no longer consumes his attention. Another reality seizes him. Fear now fills his heart and the rest is history.

The greater the storm, the greater the miracle needed; in such cases, to secure the victory, the more intense your concentration must be on Christ. Be assured that Jesus is enough to guarantee your triumph. Keep your eyes upon Him, "Looking unto Jesus, the author and finisher of your faith." (Hebrews 12:2)

———•·•———

The Bloody-Nose Sermon

"...Eleazar,...one of the three mighty men with Da-
vid, when they defied the Philistines that were there
gathered together to battle, and the men of Israel
were gone away: He arose, and smote the Philistines
until his hand was weary, and his hand clave unto
the sword: and the LORD wrought a great victory
that day; and the people returned after him only to
spoil."

(2 Samuel 23:9-10)

*O*ften, what makes for triumph, victory and greatness
is perseverance. Discouragement knocks at the door
of every heart and often finds its lodging. Through vigilance
and perseverance, we could make it an uncomfortable guest
and oust it from our midst. Eleazar, by the example of his
testimony, lends us encouragement not to give up at even
the weariest of times.

This passage holds a special place in my heart, for it was
during my first time preaching from it, in the earlier time of
my ministry, that I received a true miracle. From the time of
my bible college days, I had suffered regularly with intense
bloody noses. At the time, I had a night job spray-painting
metal office furniture. From working with the lacquer-based
paint, and not wearing any facial protection, the membranes
of my nostrils were greatly weakened. Oftentimes, in the

winter months especially, my nose would bleed to such a degree that nothing I could do would get it under control and invariably I would have to get it cauterized.

A first for me was to have one of these nosebleeds during my preaching and, wouldn't you know it, it occurred while preaching on the perseverance of Eleazar from this very passage! Because the message was about never giving up, even through the most trying of circumstances, I felt it necessary to continue to preach even while I was bleeding. As I preached, the blood flowed steadily and more heavily until I was hemorrhaging. Still, I preached on, at times choking on the blood as it ran down into my throat. When I completed the approximately forty minute message, still standing before the people, I was stunned to realize that the bleeding had completely stopped.

> It has been twenty something years since that Sunday and I have not had a single nose bleed since!

"The LORD wrought a great victory that day." Well, it has been twenty-something years since that Sunday and I have not had a single nose bleed since! As I persevered through all obstacles, the Lord was gracious and faithful, proving Himself mighty in my life.

Is there a stubborn circumstance in your life that disheartens you or discourages you from going forward? Are you weary in the battle and tempted to back off? Then, may the Lord use the life of Eleazar, and my personal testimony, to strengthen you to continue in the battle in hopes of the victory that only God can bring.

The Weary Warrior
That Won A War

"...Eleazar,...one of the three mighty men with David, when they defied the Philistines that were there gathered together to battle, and the men of Israel were gone away: He arose, and smote the Philistines until his hand was weary, and his hand clave unto the sword: and the LORD wrought a great victory that day; and the people returned after him only to spoil."

(2 Samuel 23:9-10)

The story of Eleazar is phenomenal and one of my bible favorites for reasons mentioned earlier. At a time when self-pity seemed justifiable, fear irrepressible and weariness understandable, Eleazar persevered, engaging himself in the battle, trusting the Lord and conquering every foe.

Others had backed down, drawn away and given up, leaving Eleazar alone. Not only did he not allow the apathy of others to become the measure of his commitment (entering the battle when the others would not), but he remained steadfast when no one else came to his aid or rescue.

Discouragement is often the devil's device for wearing out God's precious people, causing them to give in and give up before the manifestation and realization of victory. C.S. Lewis was fond of telling an intriguing tale to illustrate this truth. He spoke of an auction that Satan held in which all of his tools were put up for sale. There was one tool, however, distinguishingly marked "not for sale," separating it from the others. When asked what that tool was and why it was not for sale, Satan responded, "That is the tool of discouragement. By it, I can accomplish all my work." Discouragement has always been the greatest device of the enemy. All who will live godly in Christ Jesus, pursuing lofty goals and engaging in God's work, will be subject to times of weariness intensified by discouragement. Eleazar was no exception. Somewhere, perhaps at the half-way point, when the initial enthusiasm and excitement of an endeavor first begins to wear off, and the end seems still a great way off, and no sign of completion is in view, despair often gets the best of us. This is the weary point. Here, a decision must be made. This is the time when you can readily feel sorry for yourself and succumb to despair, or a new determination and resolve can carry you beyond the weary point to triumph and victory. Here, Eleazar, defying all feeling and thought, grips his sword one more time to engage in battle. It is at this moment of decision and determination that faith is at its purest and finest.

It is always easier to let discouragement get the best of us than it is to stand against the things that weary us, but the promise is to the overcomer. The turning point for Eleazar came, when at the weary point, he stood his ground, cleaving to his sword. It was in direct response to this resolve that the Lord's strength was made manifest.

Eleazar means "God is my helper" and surely God was, but He is the helper of all who do not draw back in the day of adversity. He will show Himself faithful as we trust Him in every respect. Has He not said that if you believe, then you would see the glory of God? May you trust Him, Who has promised His aid and victory in all things, today.

New Strength

"But they that wait upon the LORD shall renew their strength; they shall mount up with wings as eagles; they shall run, and not be weary; and they shall walk, and not faint."

(Isaiah 40:31)

*A*ll human strength is derived strength. All things on earth are in need of renewal. How much more our spirits, which are completely dependent on God for their sustenance? Most people never recognize this fact and go about thinking they are standing by their own powers. As Christians, however, we are quite aware of the infusion of divine power into our lives. Though God's strength is never diminished, we must not be surprised when our resources are depleted. The human heart is not replenished with sleep; the human body is, but not the human spirit. Only God's Presence can renew the heart.

On a daily basis we are tested and taxed from three sides. The world, the flesh and the devil combine to deplete the resources we enjoy from the life of God within us. We stand in need of replenishing and renewal. We must not get discouraged over the fact that we cannot, of ourselves, sustain a continued strength. The words of Phillipp Melancthon, Luther's companion, spoken centuries ago, ring true in each of our hearts: "Old Adam is too strong for young Melancthon." We are dependent on God for new mercies. The promise is that His supply is vast and His heart is willing to share His power and presence with you. You need only to avail yourselves of His help. He is ready, willing and able to visit those who wait on Him.

He is more interested in your weakness than He is in your strength today, more apt to help you in what you cannot do than in what you are able to do. In fact, the word that is used for "renew" means "exchange." When we come into the presence of God we exchange our weakness for His strength. That is to say that through worship, our weakness is surrendered and His reviving power comes to us. We lose our inability and draw from His omnipotence.

Our message is simple: Depend on God and He will graciously sustain you. Nothing baffles Him; He is hindered only by our independence. A strong people are a people dependent on God. His delight is to continually empower and refresh you. The promise is that as we wait upon Him, that is, look to Him with hopeful and eager anticipation, we shall stretch our wings forth and be lifted up as eagles. Eagles are known for their ability to soar readily and with ease. From these moments of rapture, we gain the strength to run without tiring and the ability to walk without despairing.

Perhaps you are weary. Perhaps you are disheartened by

> When we come into the presence of God we exchange our weakness for His strength

your own failures and despondency, having expected better things of yourself. This is not a time to count on your depleted resources or look to your failing condition. This is the hour of the Lord's power and visitation in your life. Hold your head up. Look unto Him from whence cometh your help.

———•◆•———

Big-Mouthed Believers

"I am the LORD thy God, which brought thee out of the land of Egypt: open thy mouth wide, and I will fill it."

(Psalm 81:10)

Certainly you have seen, at least in photographs, new-born baby birds awaiting food from their mothers. It seems these young ones are all mouths. Their wide-open mouths speak, not only of their great appetites, but also of their desperate dependence. Our Father delights to fill the mouths of the hungry and to satisfy those who depend on Him. So our text encourages our desire and our appeal toward Him for full satisfaction. This spiritual hunger of heart is the divine prerequisite and, in fact, the only spiritual qualification for God's manifest blessing. "Blessed are the poor in spirit, for theirs is the kingdom of heaven" are the first words of teaching that Jesus brings in the New Testament.

However, the promise of God's speedy response to an inclination and desire for Him is not all that is communicated in this text. Here, the Lord wants His people to be assured of His willingness to bless them to such an extent that they would approach Him without fear and timidity. The death of Jesus on our behalf has swung the door of Heaven wide open for us. We are invited to come boldly before the throne of grace to obtain mercy and help for all of our needs. This opening of the mouth wide is an edict for God's people to approach Him boldly. We face not an angry judge, but a benevolent Lord, completely ready to respond to our request. Stop deeming yourself unworthy. Stop imagining that you will be brushed aside. Come as though you have the right to come, for this you do, by what He has done for you.

Additionally, these words, "Open your mouth wide and I will fill it," deal with the size and extent of our request. One of the most quoted, but misunderstood, verses of scripture is Ephesians 3:20. Here, Paul speaks of "Him that is able to do exceedingly, abundantly, above all we ask or think." This verse is often used to say that God's blessing will exceed our expectations and imaginations. Thankfully, He often does overtake us with unexpected and unimaginable abundance. However, this verse is not about what God will do beyond our expectation, but of what He will do in direct response to our expectation. Paul does not say, "God will do." He actually says "He is able to do." This verse, along with the ones before it, is a call to enlarge our vision, pursuit, and quest. It is asking us to greater comprehend and ascertain God's boundless love, willingness and ability to bestow His goodness in our lives. The Word here urges us to increase our expectation and expand our anticipation of God's bounty. The inference is that we should enlarge and expand our requests to rise to the level of the Lord's willingness to

> Come as though you have the right to come, for this you do, by what He has done for you

bestow. "We have not, because we ask not." (James 4:2)

Further, this great text demonstrates God's willingness to bless His people from the glorious redemption that He has wrought on our behalf. He has taken us out of bondage, darkness and destruction, choosing us as His very own; surely, nothing is too great to ask of Him! He brought us out so that He might bring us in. Anticipate a great manifestation of God in your life, today.

———•◆•———

Because He Lives

"For I delivered unto you first of all that which I also received, how that Christ died for our sins according to the scriptures; And that he was buried, and that he rose again the third day according to the scriptures:"

(1 Corinthians 15:3-4)

The central doctrine of Christianity has its foundation in the death of Jesus. It is the death of Jesus that atones for our sins. God forbid that we should ever minimize the cross of Christ. The death of Jesus is assuredly the foundation of blessings for the church. It is upon the cross that the price was paid and the way is made for our acceptance and peace with God. Here, the door of grace is opened for us. Yet, remarkably, the death of Jesus was not the central event in the life of the New Testament church! They did not, early on, glory in the death of Christ. Jesus' dying was not something they rejoiced in, nor would have, apart from His subsequent resurrection and visitation. When Jesus died, His disciples scattered. Their dreams were shattered and their hopes were dashed. With the death of Jesus, for all practical purposes, any notion of "Christianity" or a "church" faded into oblivion. There was no intention on the part of His fol-

lowers to continue to gather or carry any message of His forward, once He was gone. Far from being eager enthusiasts to
perpetuate His cause, they were unwilling to accept any
news or testimony of His resurrection. After committing all
to Him, only to be apparently deserted in the end, the disciples were extremely hesitant and reluctant to believe.

The early church was founded upon the miraculous.
For some forty days after His death, until the time of His
ascension, Jesus showed Himself alive, only to return again
in the person of the Holy Spirit on
the day of Pentecost (the Holy Spirit
being nothing less than the manifest
presence of the risen Jesus). The
early church was established and
sustained by a firsthand knowledge
and experience of the resurrected
Christ. They exulted and gloried in

> The death of
> Jesus was not the
> central event in
> the life of the New
> Testament Church

a Jesus who was indeed alive. They assembled and went forth
in a knowledge that He was with them in a powerful way.
They were witnesses of His resurrection by and through the
Holy Spirit. This is truly what empowered the first century
Christians. This is what altered their lives and the lives of
those with whom they came into contact. There is no understanding or explaining the New Testament church without
the reality of the resurrected Jesus and His glorious presence
in the midst of His people.

I sometimes wonder and fear that if Jesus were not
alive, and the Holy Spirit were not poured forth, that many
churches today would continue with business as usual! Their
teaching would go on uninterrupted and whatever life they

seem to have would perpetuate itself, undisturbed. There is a sort of Christless Christianity that exists in many a church.

The cross is the gateway blessing of the New Covenant. Indeed, it is the primary blessing, but as such it is but a means to an end. The goal of the atonement is that God might share His life with us. This He does through the infilling of the Holy Spirit. He died so that we might have life. He gave Himself *for* us so that He might give Himself *to* us. Christianity is more than any teaching about Jesus. It is more than following the example of our Lord. It is more than the fact that He died to take away our sins. Christianity is having the life of God in us. Jesus is alive and His people are experiencing His life. May you, through His resurrection, experience His life and presence, today!

Forgiving and Forgiveness

"For if ye forgive men their trespasses, your heavenly Father will also forgive you: But if ye forgive not men their trespasses, neither will your Father forgive your trespasses."

(Matthew 6:14-15)

*I*n saying "if ye forgive men their trespasses, your heavenly Father will also forgive you," our Lord seems to indicate that forgiving others is the grounds or the means of receiving forgiveness for oneself. He takes it further by powerfully declaring that if we do not forgive others, neither can we be forgiven.

In order to properly understand the Bible, it is important to compare scripture with scripture and to interpret the less clear and more obscure passages of the Bible in the light of those things that are most clearly presented and certainly understood. It is a fundamental biblical truth, accepted by all Evangelical Christians, that our forgiveness is the free gift of God, completely unmerited by any doing of our own. This being the clearly presented truth of scripture, we must understand what Jesus is saying here so as not to contradict this foundational doctrine. Whatever this need to forgive others signifies, it cannot mean that we earn our forgiveness by forgiving.

The scriptures teach that faith in God's grace is the foundation of our acceptance with God and the means of His favor in our lives. It is faith alone that saves, yet, as Calvin said, "The faith that saves is not alone." Faith brings grace and grace is transforming. True faith causes God's graces to flow and work themselves into the human heart. Love and forgiveness are among these graces. The person who is unwilling to love or forgive is evidencing that grace has not entered his/her life or is resisting the flow of grace and thereby diminishing and/or severing the reception of future grace to their lives. As we allow the grace of forgiveness to flow in and through us, we are both confirming the fact that we are the recipient of God's grace and are also keeping our hearts in a condition conducive to the reception of future grace. A willingness to forgive, or possessing a spirit of forgiveness, is a tangible proof or manifestation of faith. Forgiveness demonstrates that faith is operative and genuine. Unforgiveness reveals the opposite. It verifies that there is a lack of genuine faith, hindering the flow of grace in an individual's life. The principle here is that present grace, as received by true biblical faith, is the precursor and guarantee of future grace. As we respond to the Lord's leading, through grace, we meet the condition of receptivity for future grace. So it is not contradictory, but complementary to the doctrine of justification by grace through faith to say, "Forgive, and you shall be forgiven" (Luke 6:37). The believer must be willing to forgive, for the ability to forgive is the fruit and evidence of faith. An unfor-

> Possessing a spirit of forgiveness is a manifestation of faith

giving believer becomes an oxymoron, or at least a dysfunc-
tional believer, shutting down the free flow of divine grace.

If you can grasp this truth, you are nearer to an understanding of what Jesus meant when He said, "To him that
has, more shall be given, but to him that has not, it shall be
taken away even that which he seems to have" (Matthew
13:12). As our living faith allows God's grace to have full
sway in our lives, we open ourselves up to an influx of more
grace and, in so doing, we bring to pass the promise of "grace
upon grace."

To Forgive or
Not To Forgive?

"Then Peter came to Jesus and asked, "Lord, how many times shall I forgive my brother when he sins against me? Up to seven times? Jesus answered, "I tell you, not seven times, but seventy times seven."
(Matthew 18:21-22)

ere, the Lord clearly tells us that forgiveness is not optional; it is required! We cannot pick and choose where and when we will forgive. Significantly, Jesus does not say that we are to forgive based on the repentance or change of heart of the offender. We must practice forgiveness despite continued and repeated ill behaviors towards us. The reason for this is that as believers we cannot afford the price of unforgiveness. Indeed, there are consequences that come to the human spirit as a result of an unwillingness to forgive.

In speaking to his cabinet on the evening before his resignation, President Richard Nixon may have said it best when he stated that "There will be those that hate you, but they cannot destroy you unless you hate them and thereby destroy yourself." The primary reason we must practice forgiveness is not for the good of the one forgiven, but for the preservation and fruitfulness of our own spiritual condition.

Anger, resentment and bitterness occupy space in the human heart and hinder the free flow of divine grace. In forgiving our offenders, we are releasing any polluted and poisonous thoughts from occupying our time, thoughts and heart.

Many struggle with this call to forgiveness, imagining that forgiveness demands reconciliation. The two, however, are not synonymous. While it is impossible to have reconciliation without forgiveness, it is quite possible to have forgiveness without reconciliation. The principle here is that, while forgiveness must be in place regardless of any positive action on the part of the offender, reconciliation requires a change of heart and action on the part of the one that has caused the offense.

The call to forgiveness does not require our continued willful subjection to repeated acts of offense, hurt and abuse. In fact, we should not continue deep and intimate relationships with those that assault us with persistent, unrepentant and unrelenting offensive behaviors. John F. Kennedy once wittingly said, "Forgive your enemies, but remember their names."

> It is quite possible to have forgiveness without reconciliation

Forgiveness always, hope continuously, and reconciliation whenever possible are the scriptural principles. Hence the words, "Love believes all things; hopes all things" and the mandate, "As much as possible, seek to live peaceably with all men." That is, look to believe in and see the best in all people and hope for the most excellent possible outcome to every conflict.

Our forgiveness can, in fact, be redemptive. It may be the means that God uses to bring about a change of heart in an individual. May His grace so work in our hearts that we are enabled to fulfill this divine precept.

———•◆•———

The Rare Jewel of Contentment

"Let your conversation be without covetousness; and be content with such things as ye have: for he hath said, I will never leave thee, nor forsake thee. So that we may boldly say, The Lord is my helper..."
(Hebrews 13:5-6)

The word "conversation" is Old English and represents more than just mere words used while speaking. The word addresses attitude and manner of living. It includes how we talk and the things we say, but goes deeper and further to include our way of thinking and mindset. The instruction here, negatively stated, admonishes us to avoid a covetous heart; positively, it speaks to us of contentment in what we presently possess.

We need not, and ought not, live a life characterized, controlled or centered in a sense of lack and want. At the heart of covetousness lies a longing or lusting for things not possessed. The covetous heart is discontent, feeling a lack of things considered vital.

In contrast to the covetous heart is the contented life. Contentment is a satisfaction arising from appreciating and prizing what is presently in our grasp; a heart gladdened by what is at hand.

Covetousness will always manifest itself in grumbling and complaining. Contentment, on the other hand, ushers in a thankful spirit, filled with a sense of gratitude. But here, we are given the secret as to how we may secure and maintain contentment and escape the grip of a covetous heart. In telling us to be content in what we possess, the writer seizes the occasion to remind his readers that whatever it is they may feel they are lacking, they have the Lord and His steadfast love

> A lively faith in God is truly the grounds of contentment in our lives

and promises. He never abandons or fails! He is an ever present and faithful provider of all we need. Awareness and a lively appreciation of this fact establishes contentment in the heart and causes confidence to emerge in the soul. Discontentment and covetousness, along with an accompanying grumbling heart, come as a result of forgetting and neglecting the great fact that God is with us. Having a lively faith in God is truly the grounds of contentment in our lives. A sense of anticipation arises when faith is operative. A knowledge that His hand provides all that we need floods the heart of those who trust Him.

Notice how the phrase "He hath said," of verse 5, results in the declaration "that we may boldly say," of verse 6. Our confidence springs forth from His nature and promise. Over against your fears and imaginations, "He hath said!" Will you believe His heart and revelation or the devil's lie and your vain thoughts?

Today, you need not wallow in a feeling of being forgotten nor be distracted by any apparent advantage that another may have over you. You have, with you and for you, the Lord who never abandons, deserts or fails. Oh what satisfaction arises from recognizing God as our present and perpetual portion! You have everything you need today. You have Him!

———•·•———

Delay, Not Denial

"And he spake a parable unto them to this end, that men ought always to pray, and not to faint; Saying, There was in a city a judge, which feared not God, neither regarded man."

(Luke 18:1-2)

We needn't guess at the purpose of the parable of the importunate widow and the unjust judge. It is clearly stated in the first verse of Luke 18. Here, we are told that Jesus spoke this parable to encourage men to persist in prayer and not lose heart. Those who maintain a lively prayer life of faith and communion with God will not faint. Those who are fainting are the ones who have faltered in their confident expression of faith through prayer. Jesus' purpose in likening the church to a widow seeking justice and vindication, only to be put off for a season, is to enforce the truth that those who will ultimately prevail must overcome the difficulty presented through delay. In fact, "fainting" is the direct consequence of an inability to sustain a belief in the goodness and imminence of God amidst a season of delay.

While the purpose of the parable is quite clear, the point intended by the figure of an unrighteous, reluctant, disinterested and merciless judge is less easily discerned. It is quite apparent that Jesus did not intend to portray our heavenly Father as uncaring and callous to our concerns. In fact, the New Testament picture of God is one of a merciful, gracious, benevolent and loving Father who goes to great lengths to save, deliver and bless His children.

If God is nothing like the unjust judge of the parable, then why did Jesus employ this figure? Why not, instead, speak of a righteous and compassionate judge with whom the woman in need finds favor; one who is sympathetic to her cause and takes up her concern? This is not merely an interesting question, but one that speaks to the heart of the intent of the parable. The point that Jesus wishes to make is that those

> Those that are willing to settle for less are guaranteed nothing at all!

who are to be triumphant must overcome the temptation, through God's delayed response, to imagine that He is truly reluctant, indifferent, cold and calloused toward them. Faith, manifesting itself in victorious praying, does not accept the feeling of being despised by God because of delay. It does not fall into the trap of thinking that God must somehow be squeezed into doing things He isn't inclined to do. True prayer is the voice of faith that lays hold of God's willingness to answer prayer despite imaginations of His reluctance that present themselves through delay. Although the reason for delay is never given, and oftentimes remains a mystery, the triumphant believer persists in prayer recognizing God's resolve to visit and bless His people. Faith knows the heart and mind of God beyond His withheld hand.

A further point of the parable seems to be that God

promises only to respond to insistent and persistent prayer. Those that are willing to settle for less are guaranteed nothing at all! These are the fainting ones. The true faith and prayer that Jesus advocates and honors is tireless. It is certain of God's willingness and sure of God's answer.

God's delays are not denials. He is not slack concerning His promises. Days you yearn for are coming soon. Stand strong in faith and prayer. The Lord delights in answering the cry of His people.

———•◆•———

Impossibility,
Not Probability

"Who against hope believed in hope, that he might become the father of many nations, according to that which was spoken, So shall thy seed be. And being not weak in faith, he considered not his own body now dead, when he was about an hundred years old, neither yet the deadness of Sarah's womb: He staggered not at the promise of God through un- belief; but was strong in faith, giving glory to God."
(Romans 4:18-20)

*I*n an attempt to illustrate faith, I've heard it said that when someone sits down on a chair, faith that the chair will support them is exercised, or when someone rides in a bus, faith is exercised believing that the bus will get them to their destination. In reality, all such examples of "faith," demonstrate confidence in probability through the mathe- matical law of averages, rather than faith. I believe the chair will hold me because it has in the past; I believe that the bus will get me to my desired destination because it has a solid history of doing so on a regular basis. This is not the same as the biblical faith spoken of when it comes to believing for the miraculous.

Miracles, by their very nature, defy the law of averages and are not at all based on likelihood and probability. The faith required for miracles is not arrived at by rational processes of the mind, but is born and developed in the heart. Faith is a spiritual confidence in God and His Word that comes through the revelation of Himself to the human heart. It is founded upon His goodness, faithfulness and omnipotence.

It was "against hope," that is without the least ground in the realm of sense or reason to find hope or expectation, where Abraham found himself when the promise came. One word characterized the natural likelihood or probability of Sarah bearing a child: Impossible! Another word characterized the natural feeling in Abraham's heart: Hopeless!

Miracles by their nature defy the law of averages

The promise of God to Abraham was "staggering." In other words, it was mind-boggling. It was astounding. It was shocking. It made absolutely no sense from a natural standpoint. Yet, from a natural or logical standpoint, it was precisely when it would have been madness to hope, that Abraham believed. He "staggered not" at the promise of God. Faith is not irrational, but it is often supra-rational in its exercise. That is, not against reason, but above and beyond reason. His confidence was not in possibilities or probabilities, but in God. His faith was unmoved by the physical condition of his and Sarah's bodies. He counted them as irrelevant to the fulfilling of the promise. Trusting God, Abraham did not look back. His sole consideration had become God and His promise. These he kept in the highest regard and thus he was strengthened in faith. As he glorified God, his faith was "filled to the brim" (as the word "strengthened" means in the original Greek). All such confidence brings glory to God and honors His integrity.

We need not look to the probability or natural likelihood of events transpiring to foster or boost our faith. In fact, natural appearances often dissuade belief in the promises. Only as we exalt God and His Word over natural facts, projections and feelings are we truly standing in faith and glorifying God. God is not limited to doing those things that are probable or naturally possible in our lives. Perhaps, even now, you are facing a situation that is improbable or even impossible. The God you serve is master over the impossible. Take the limit off Him and believe Him today!

———•◆•———

All Care All Prayer

"Be careful for nothing; but in every thing by prayer and supplication with thanksgiving let your requests be made known unto God. And the peace of God, which passeth all understanding, shall keep your hearts and minds through Christ Jesus."
(Philippians 4:6-7)

I suppose to be human is to be anxious. Anxiety and consuming care are a part of our lives because many things we encounter are larger than us and beyond our control. It is easy for the care-free to challenge the care-filled, saying, "What are you worrying about?" "Everything is going to be all right. Cheer up!" Such counsel is futile, lacking compassion and provides no promise of hope or prescription for victory.

Paul, himself, had great reason for anxious care, being imprisoned and facing an uncertain future at the time of this writing. Yet, Paul tells us not to be anxious. This he does by providing a proven path to overcoming consuming concerns and obtaining God's peace.

Life is, indeed, uncertain and at times can be too great for us. The word "worry," at its root, means "to strangle or to choke." The Greek word for "careful" means "to pull in different directions so as to stretch thin or tear up." "Peace" is the polar opposite of anxiety and speaks of a sense of well-being and connotes a feeling of safety. The word itself means "wholeness" and refers to something "intact" or "that which is held together." So then, those who are anxious are being torn to pieces while those who have peace are being held together!

In these two verses, Paul tells us how we may go from "consuming care" to "perfect peace;" how, in fact, peace can come and conquer care in our lives. The peace promised does not arise from external circumstances, but it is an internal and spiritual state of the heart that can be had in any situation.

Prayer is the biblical prescription for conquering care. The key to victory is found in the word, "but." "But" means rather, instead of, better yet or as an alternative to. So then, Paul says rather than being "careful," instead of being torn up and overwhelmed by consuming care, or, as an alternative and antidote to care, practice prayer. In prayer we take the things that gnaw at our minds and bring

> Prayer is much more than telling God our problems; it is making Him our solution!

them to God. We take our concerns and those things that are too great for us to Him who is greatly concerned about us and for whom nothing is too great. Our cares are the raw materials of which our prayers are made. "In everything" depicts the scope of prayer, that is, in every situation we find ourselves, in every care and concern that comes to us, these are the things that we need to make the matter of prayer.

What is on the mind should be on the heart. "Thanksgiving" shows the confidence to be had in prayer. Praise keeps our prayer positive for prayer is much more than telling God our problems; it is making Him our solution! It is coming confidently to the One that is baffled by nothing, including our own sin, and acknowledging Him as our source of sustenance and well-being.

Indeed, anxiety in the life of the believer is the accumulation of concerns not carried to Christ. May you bring Him your petitions now and may you find His peace.

———•·•———

Peace In Possession

"And the peace of God, which passeth all under-standing, shall keep your hearts and minds through Christ Jesus."

(Philippians 4:7)

The alternative to anxious, consuming care is a perfect peace that comes as a direct result of the practice of God's presence through prayer. As we transfer the control of our concerns from our personal care and self-reliance, through a trusting dependence upon the Lord and His sovereign goodness, the peace of God becomes ours.

This peace is said to transcend our understanding. This is often taken to mean that it is inexplicable. It is known in the experience of it, but it is impossible to put into terms. However, it also means much more than this. In saying that this peace "passes all understanding," Paul is saying that it is not something that is produced merely by our reasoning and way of thinking.

Indeed, anxiety is a work of the mind. It is born of projection. In other words, it is the consequence of a worrisome outlook on an uncertain future that is beyond our control. Yet the peace God gives, and Paul describes, is not simply achieved by a change in thinking. It is experienced and imparted through direct and immediate communication with God. It is in this sense that it is said to "passeth all understanding." It does not have its origin in rational processes of the human mind; it has its origin in God. It is not a peace concocted through positive thoughts, but a peace imparted by God's Spirit. It is not imaginary nor is it irrational. It is supra-rational. It is beyond and above reason in its origin. It is the direct result of the hand of God that is experienced through communion with God.

This peace does not necessarily predict or forecast a precise outcome to all of our particular circumstances, but it does grant a supernatural sense of complete composure. As we take the anxious cares that surmount in our minds and overwhelm us to the God who is overwhelmed and baffled by nothing, our thoughts are calmed by the communication of His Spirit to our hearts. Through He who is greater than us and infinite in nature, we are taken from the frantic fear of our undoing and demise to a stabilized posture of confidence in His loving concern and assured provision. An unruffled serenity and an incomprehensible sense of safety and assurance become ours. Though we know not what tomorrow holds, we know who holds tomorrow. Our hearts and minds find rest as we are overtaken by serenity and an overall sense that "it is well."

> Though we know not what tomorrow holds, we know Who holds tomorrow

Through this process of communication of ourselves to God and God to ourselves, peace takes possession of the heart and mind. Interestingly and importantly, the word "keep" is a military term denoting, first of all, a "conquering" of our thoughts and feelings through the triumph of God in our hearts and minds. God's peace overtakes and conquers our anxiety. Secondly, it speaks of a "guarding" and "protecting" of that which has been conquered. God's peace is a garrison: an occupying, defensive force against the rule of all anxiety.

May this conquering and protecting peace be yours even now as you pray.

———•◦•———

Being Before Doing

"And he ordained twelve, that they should be with him, and that he might send them forth to preach."
(Mark 3:14)

*T*he great theme of the Gospels is the coming of God's Son to secure the salvation of mankind. While recognizing this, it is also important to understand that the central message of the covenant is not, "I will forgive them," but "I will be with them." "I will be their God and they shall be my people" is the repeated Old Testament prophecy of the coming New Testament. Indeed, forgiveness is the necessary and fundamental blessing of the Covenant, but salvation is much more than the forgiveness of our sins. Salvation is union and fellowship with the Father, through the Son, by the Spirit. Forgiveness is the means to that end. It is the "gateway blessing." It opens the door to every other blessing and to the fulfillment of God's intention; to dwell with us and to glorify Himself. The price for our sins has been satisfied, thereby restoring us and allowing us to become partakers of the divine life. It is through this union, communion and fellowship with God that we are transformed into His likeness.

It is highly significant that when Jesus chose the disciples who would later become His apostles, His first intention was that they "should be with Him." Indeed, His ultimate plan was that 'He might send them forth" and that they might be used mightily. However, His first purpose was that they would be with Him. Intimacy is the primary thing, service is secondary. Relationship takes precedence over ministry. In fact, relationship is the foundation of ministry. "Being" is the qualification for "doing."

The amazing thing about the disciples (and all other great men of the bible for that matter) is that, in themselves, they were all remarkably unremarkable. Indeed, they became noteworthy, but they were not naturally or initially so. They were extraordinarily ordinary until God had His way with them. They were as rough stones until transformed into the image of Christ.

> Intimacy is the primary thing, service is secondary

Interestingly, the Greek word used in the New Testament to speak of transformation is the word from which we get the word metamorphosis. Metamorphosis describes the changing from one state or condition to another. We use the word to describe the process of the caterpillar becoming the butterfly. It further signifies a work done from the inside out (the outer fashion or manifestation taking shape from the nature within). So we read of Jesus being transfigured before them on the mount. As we spend time with God, we are transformed. We take on His likeness and are changed from the inside out. A new heart has become ours in Christ. His Spirit and likeness take up residence inside of us and prove life changing. It is this new nature within us that qualifies and equips us for ministry.

Our greatest privilege and calling is to live our lives in the sweet fellowship and enjoyment of God. Jesus died to secure this union and communion. Indeed, the love of the Father flows through the blood of the Son and is experienced by means of the Holy Spirit. Our first and highest calling is always a participation in this union and fellowship. From this, we are prepared to minister and reflect God's glory. May you enjoy and serve Him now.

Have Thine Own Way

"And He ordained twelve, that they should be with Him, and that He might send them forth to preach."
(Mark 3:14)

The Apostles of the Book of Acts seem so unlike the disciples of the gospels. What men of God they had become! Jesus wisely did not leave His church in the hands of just anybody, but in those who had spent time with Him most regularly and had surrendered themselves to Him most thoroughly. Three-plus years of daily walking with the Master had paid great dividends. As these men came under Christ's teaching and touch, their lives were radically transformed. He had truly made them "fishers of men."

No matter what our vocation or ambitions, our universal calling is to glorify God. This is accomplished as we yield ourselves to Him. In a day when most want God to move for them, and many wish God would do more through them, what God is seeking are those who will allow Him to do more in them! Before He ever releases His own to minister and sends them forth to preach, He bids them to sit, learn and grow. Apprenticeship with Christ is the qualification of ministry for Christ. Need we be reminded that "ministry" is meant to glorify Him and not promote ourselves? If we ever truly hope to work for God, we must walk *with* God. We are ambassadors and as such, are commissioned to bear the message of another and to reflect His person. Discipleship is the qualification for apostleship.

Each of the disciples, with the exception of Judas Iscariot, of course, underwent a complete metamorphosis as they submitted themselves to Christ. He shaped and molded their thinking and lives, not merely by association, but by impartation. Through being with Him, the Holy Spirit was at work fashioning the hearts and lives of His followers after His likeness. I think of James and John who were known as the "Sons of Thunder" in the early ministry of Christ. Being unlearned in His ways, they were eager to call fire down from Heaven. Yet, in spite of this, years later John was to be recognized as the apostle of love. What a transformation he experienced, being with Jesus!

> We glorify God most when we most closely resemble Him

We glorify God most when we most closely resemble Him. Our greatest calling is to be with Him. He desires to communicate Himself to others through us. This He does as we draw closer to Him in personal devotion. I've often heard it said that the only "ability" that the Lord looks for is "availability," but I have discovered that what He really wants is more than this. Indeed, the Lord desires teachability, liability and humility. As you spend time in God's presence today, may you ask Him not only to work for you and through you, but also ask Him to do His greatest work in you.

———•◦•———

Day and Night

"And the same day, when the even was come, He saith unto them, Let us pass over unto the other side."

(Mark 4:35)

*E*very word of the scriptures is significant and, often times, that which is casually passed over contains much meaning and insight. Such is the case in point with today's reading. In recording the events of this storm, Mark begins by asserting that it was the evening of the same day that Jesus had instructed His disciples by the parable of the seed and the soils. What a blessed day it must have been to sit in the presence of the Lord and to hear Him teach the great truths of His Kingdom as He expounded His ways with such wisdom. That day, our Lord reminded His followers that the seed of the Word of God must meet with favorable conditions in the soil of the human heart if it is to penetrate, germinate and bear fruit. The condition of the soil plays a significant part in the productivity of the seed. The disciples were those who, having heard the word, received it with the promise of bearing great fruit.

Now it is evening and the disciples will have a perfect opportunity in which to employ and demonstrate the faith sown in their hearts by the Word they heard that very afternoon! The excitement and enthusiasm they experienced on the calm shore that day, as they listened to earth's greatest teacher, would be sorely tried and tested in the stormy deep of the night. Not unlike us, the disciples forgot in the night what they had received and learned in the day.

It is one thing to believe and rejoice in the sunshine of the day; it is another to trust Him unwaveringly in the dark and stormy night. It is one thing to believe Him in church, while we are being stirred by corporate singing and encouraged by the preaching of the Word; it is another to continue to praise Him, believe Him and trust Him as we come up against the world and life's circumstances as they assail us. Indeed, the disciples' faith was real, but many times, believing goes out the window when problems arise and present themselves. It is not that the disciples are NOT believers, it is that, at the time of severe testing, they fail to recall that they ARE believers! They certainly thought highly of their Master, but at the moment of peril, they did not think of their Master at all! They were immediately taken by the storm at sea and it so clamored for their time and attention that they failed to properly consider Christ. They left God out at precisely the time when they needed most to bring Him in! They were filled with care and not filled with prayer. The peril had brought panic and they permitted panic to rule their hearts and minds.

> It is not that the disciples are NOT believers, it is that, at the time of severe testing, they fail to recall that they ARE believers!

We also often face situations that seize our hearts and minds so as to make us forget that we are believers and Whom it is that is with us. May you now, in whatever situation you find yourself in remember that you are kept by the power of God and safe with Christ in the boat.

———•••———

It's a Pity

"One who was there had been an invalid for thirty-eight years. When Jesus saw him lying there and learned that he had been in this condition for a long time, he asked him, "Do you want to get well?" "Sir," the invalid replied, "I have no one to help me…"
(John 5:5-7 NIV)

*O*n the surface, it appears to be a silly question to ask a man, lame for thirty-eight years, if he wishes to be made well. Yet things (and life for that matter) are often not as simple as they appear. The complexity of the issue is evident in the answer this man gives to Jesus. His reply is not to say immediately, "Certainly." He does not say, as we might expect, "Of course I want to be made whole. That is the very reason I am here!" No, the answer is more telling than that and helps us to understand the wisdom and significance of the question in the first place. "Sir," he says, "I have no one to help me…" I can sense the pathos of despair resounding in that reply. I hear the voice of self-sorrow here. A voice, if we are to be completely honest, with which we are all too familiar. Jesus knows that the unrelieved condition of thirty-eight years may take a toll on the best of men.

This text speaks to all who have suffered disappointing

and debilitating setbacks. The challenge comes to us just as it came to this man. Jesus' query is to ascertain precisely how much life, faith and hope remains when death has done its best to latch itself on to us. The question comes to us to see whether despondency has gotten the better part of us and dried up our spirits, or whether the faith that connects us with Christ and hope takes up residence in our hearts. Jesus wishes to see exactly to what degree our hardships have crippled our spirits.

The man's answer is telling. It depicts the crushed hopes under which he labors and the pessimistic spirit that have gotten the better part of himself. When Jesus asks him if he wants to get well, the implication is that of course he wishes to get well, but the objection arises as to any possibility or probability of such wholeness, given his lot in life. "I have no one to help me," he says. He cries, "Foul. Life has been unfair and unkind to me. I never get a break." The seeds of self-pity have not only sprouted in his heart, but have apparently become deep rooted. He has become so consumed by his overwhelming difficulties that he no longer entertains any real hope for achievement or improvement.

> Indulgence in wallowing leads to an unbelieving and hopeless heart

His sitting by the pool has become nothing more than a ritualistic routine without any real anticipation or expectation. So strong is his despair that he is unmoved at first by even the word and presence of Christ.

Self-pity and despondency, through life's delays and withholdings, tend to deaden our own spirits. Indulgence in wallowing leads to an unbelieving and hopeless heart. God is a mountain-mover and a way-maker. May self-sorrow and self-pity be thrust far from your heart today. May you rise up to trust Him now against all lies and imaginations to the contrary.

———•+•———

Present Though Absent

"And when even was [now] come, his disciples went down unto the sea and entered into a ship, and went over the sea toward Capernaum. And it was now dark, and Jesus was not come to them."

(John 6:16-17)

*W*hile John's gospel contains no parables per se, in a very real sense John utilizes the miracles of Jesus as parabolic forms of instruction. The case in point is no exception and is full of spiritual value for the present day believer.

Although this is not the first storm the disciples ever faced, it differs greatly in one respect from prior endangerments. Whereas in the first recorded storm Jesus was present throughout, in this time of peril He is remarkably absent. John powerfully reinforces this truth by saying, literally, "Darkness had already come. Jesus had not yet come." The scene is thrust before us. "Darkness, YES; Jesus, NO!" Matthew tells us that the boat was now "distressed" (coming apart). More distressed, I suppose, were the disciples!

There is a great truth to be learned here, relative to the "sensible presence" of God and faith. While we have great promises assuring us of Christ's union and mindfulness of us at all times, this is not to say that we will always feel

His presence in our lives. While union with Christ is the foundation of our communion with Christ, this does not guarantee unchangeable feelings of fellowship. There is truly no communion without union, but union does not guarantee constant communion and a perpetual paradise. While our union with Christ is a constant, standing, verifiable fact, our communion with Him is subjective and not without its disturbances and consequent fluctuations.

The great lesson for all of Christ's disciples is in learning to trust an absent Christ, as well as a present One. We must not make our perception of His nearness (or distance) the barometer of His real interest, concern and presence. We must not allow our emotions to erroneously govern and determine our apparent position in God, but rather we must hold fast to our true position in God to harness and control our emotions. Faith is the spiritual act of appropriating the benefits of God's objective provision and translating them experientially.

> The great lesson for all of Christ's disciples is in learning to trust an absent Christ, as well as a present One

Mark tells us in his account that Jesus had gone to the mountains to pray. From His vantage point (perhaps by the light of the moon, or more likely by divine perception and revelation), He saw them toiling and rowing. Likewise, He sees us even when the darkness prohibits our seeing Him. He is there even in His perceived and apparent absence!

Take courage today. You are not the only one who struggles at times to feel God when you need Him most. He is, in fact, there and is full of compassion, concern and willingness. It is just a matter of time before He comes and steps into your situation. Weeping may endure for the night, but joy comes in the morning. In the fourth watch of the night (just about day break) Jesus came to them walking on the water. May He come to you; your situation is about to break through to victory!

———•—•———

Lost At Home

"And He said, a certain man had two sons..."
(Luke 15:11)

*U*nfortunately, the most well known parable of Jesus has mistakenly been considered primarily in relation to only ONE son. So much has been spoken and written about the "prodigal son" that it often goes unnoticed that Jesus spoke these great words about two sons.

The parable is given in response to religious murmurings over the swelling number of sinners coming to Jesus' side. The "righteous" did not comprehend how He could look so favorably and with extreme joy towards such sorts. They were adamant that the "bad" should be kept at a distance and not allowed "in." These words were not spoken primarily to the "lost ones," but to smug "insiders" who presumed themselves spiritually superior. The "elder brother" symbolically represents these "insiders." The parable, then, is about two sons. One son leaves home, tramples upon the father's love and then returns to find it; and the other son, even though he never left his father's house, remains ignorant and distant to his supreme love. Jesus sees a greater jeopardy for those who dwell in the house, being ignorant that they are distant strangers to His love, than for those wayward ones who, recognizing their forfeiture, return to receive it. Indeed, the "prodigals" were once lost, but the "religious" remain lost!

In the two sons, we see two ways of missing out on the life God has for us. One is not to understand or appreciate His love and so depart from it. The other is to be fully engaged in His service and our "doing" while never comprehending His love.

It really is a fascinating story. In it, the father's heart, having been broken by the prodigal's departure, rejoices greatly over his return, only to have his heart broken a second time by his other son.

The "lostness" of the elder brother is clearly revealed by his misunderstanding and protest when he says, "all these years have I been slaving for you and you never gave me..." Out of this intense sense of servitude, he expresses his feeling that what he has done for the father surpasses what the father ever has done for him.

> "Prodigals" were once lost, but the "religious" remain lost!

It is not that the father was unwilling to give to his son, it is that the son never understood that all that belonged to the father belonged to his child by reason of relationship. The father says, "You are ever with me and all that I have is yours." Yet, in spite of this, the son spent his years trying to live up to something that was already his! He was indeed lost at home. Though he kept all the rules, he never enjoyed the blessings and benefits of belonging. He knew nothing of the privileges and enjoyments of sonship. He was estranged from the father's love.

At last the story abruptly ends, leaving the elder son

outside on the porch. We never know for sure whether he goes in. Unfortunately, many spend the better part of their lives on the "porch." They are stuck in the struggle of a slaving, servile spirit, barring them from the full enjoyment of the privileges and benefits of sonship.

The door remains open. Let us pass today from the hardship of a slaving mentality into the joy of established sonship and join the party!

———•••———